Small Paul Wall Walker

Paul Drakeford

Copyright © 2019 Paul Drakeford

Dire Warning

This story is unsuitable for adults

and politicians.

Paul
was small

Peter
was sweeter
and Greta was neater

but Paul
was small.

They all lived together
with Big Daddy Smith
and Lucybelle.

"Lucybelle?"
I hear you exclaim.

Yes.

Mrs Liddicoat,
Lucybelle's mother, you see,
was a War baby
brought up on sheer nylon stockings
thick lipstick
the hokey pokey
and glamour.

She thought the name
Lucybelle Liddicoat
was the ant's pants.

And so it was
until her daughter married Big Daddy.
The name
Lucybelle Smith
lacked a certain
oomph!

Theirs was an average family.
They lived in the middle house
of an ordinary street
of a so so town
between somewhere
and somewhere else.

In fact the family was so average
other people came from miles around
just to see
if they were better or worse.

Who was sweeter than Peter?
Who was neater than Greta?
But Paul was smaller than all.

Once revealed
he might ruin the reputation
of this most average average family.

So Small Paul became
a very big secret.

At the first sight of a visitor
he'd be stuffed
in the wardrobe.

You can imagine
how he hated that
as the wardrobe
was full of naphthalene
and dizzy moths.

One day
while stickybeakers
were stickybeaking
through the kitchen windows,
he fell asleep.

It must have been
the naphthalene
which set the scene
for his strange dream.

He dreamt
he met
a weeny genie
in a bottle.

"Let me out of this damned bottle"
shrieked the weeny genie.

"I'm sorry. I can't hear you"
said Small Paul.
"I'll just take the cork out of this damned bottle."
Pop!
"There!
Now what was that?"

"I said take the cork out of this damned bottle.
Oh, you have already.
What a clever chap."

And the weeny genie emerged
writhing
like stale cigarette smoke
wreathed in smiles.

Once he had re-composed his dignity
he said
"Glad to get out of that.
Yes indeed indeedy.
Frightfully obliged.
Now what about some reward for your trouble
my dear fellow?
Tell me something you would really really like."

"I would really really like
to be really tall"
said Small Paul.

"Out of the question.
Quite out of the question.
You'd never fit into your clothes."

"Well couldn't I be famous
for something else?
Being small's
no fun at all."

"I know the feeling.
I was once a teeny weeny genie.
Now…
thinking…thinking…

Ah. Just the thing.
Just the thing"
said the weeny genie
leafing through his book of spells.

Then he whispered
detailed instructions
into Small Paul's ear
and quick as a wink
vanished.

Paul
awoke
tickled by moths
and confused
by the vague memory
of a bottled weeny genie,
and the slightest smell of smoke.

"I wonder if it would work"
he whispered wondering,
and obeying instructions
he bent over
and still wondering
whispered words
into his underpants.

Imagine his astonishment
when he immediately
floated into the air
and found himself
walking
on his bedroom wall.

"What a wonderful thing!
I'm a famous wall walker."

He had just walked down to the floor
when his mother
opened the bedroom door.

"Whatever have you been up to?"
she demanded
fiercely,
for there were some things
Lucybelle hated
above all else
and they were
footprints
on her walls.

"You just clean them off young man
or you'll go to bed
with no pudding."

And as he loved pudding
he did
with the tail of a shirt
dipped in the bathroom basin.

He decided
there and then
that silence was the better part of common sense
and to say nothing
about the bottle
or the weeny genie
or the spell.

And in future
he would take off his shoes
before whispering
into his underpants.

There things
may have remained
for ever and ever
but that
one day
the Prime Minister
had an idea.

He announced
to a startled House of Parliament
that he had an idea.
All the alarm bells rang
and the Opposition
woke up at once
and called for a division.

"I'm coming to that.
I'm coming to that."
said the PM
testily.

"I have decided to do something
for the average family,
and to discover the size
of the average family
we must have a division."

He summoned
his Minister for Sums
and ordered
he discover
by a process of add-ups
and a division
the size of the average family.

Within the month
he had the answer.

The average family
consisted of
one man
one wife
and
two and a half children.

The next thing
was to find out
where this average family lived.

He gave this job
to Geography George
his Minister for Geography.

George knocked on doors
up hill and down dale
stopping in strange streets,
up ugly alleys and along long lanes
asking startled citizens
some of them in dressing gowns and less
some of them still shaving
some of them putting out the cat
if they knew
or if they had seen
the average family.

Perhaps it was
Smart Alec
or Clever Dick
shaving in a dressing gown
while putting out the cat
who mentioned the address of
the Smiths
somewhere
between somewhere
and somewhere else.

Quick as three winks
Geography George skipped off
lickety split
to tell the PM.

"Fetch me my longest limo"
ordered the PM.
"I must go on a mission."

And with a packet of fresh sandwiches
and a fresh chauffeur
he was driven off
in the general direction
of somewhere else.

In the fullness of time,
and with a fullness of stomach,
he arrived at Lucybelle Smith's
and knocked.

"Good afternoon.
I'm the Prime Minister,"
he announced.
"Oh yes.
We saw you on the telly,
and you looked grand."

The PM swelled with pride
almost to the size of a grand piano.

"But not that grand"
said Lucybelle Smith.

He chose
not to notice
this unflattering addendum.

"And I have come to meet
the average family."

"That's us"
said Lucybelle,
while Mr Smith nodded,
which was all he ever got to do.

"And these are our children
Peter and Greta."

"How do you do"
said the PM
patting Peter and greeting Greta.

"Greta is sweet
and Peter's so neat.
Now tell me
is Greta sweeter than Peter
or is Peter neater than Greta?"

"No. No. No.
You have it all wrong"
expostulated Lucybelle Smith.
"Peter is sweeter
and Greta is neater."

"Yes of course.
How silly of me"
said the PM.
"Now I have it.

Let me repeat.
Peter is sweeter than Greta is neater
And Greta is fleeter than Peter's two feet.
When Peter runs faster than patients in plaster
Then Greta is beaten but neat in defeat."

Lucybelle raised one eyebrow
in disbelief.

"Who did you say you were?"
she questioned
quizzically.

"I was, and I still am,
the Prime Minister,
and I have come
to do something
for the average family.

Now let us begin.
First I must count the children.
Let me see.
One
and one
make two.

Of dear. Oh dear.
Oh deary me."
Said the PM.

"Whatever's up?"
asked Lucybelle.

"Well
I was expecting
a little extra."

"How much extra would that be?"

"Not to put too fine a point upon it,
just about, nearly, approximately,
one half extra.
You see the average family
has two and a half children."

"Well
our little extra
is in his bedroom.
You'll find him
in the wardrobe."

The PM
tiptoed
tentatively
into the bedroom
and tapped
tentatively
on the wardrobe door.

The door
slowly
creaked open.

Out flew
a squadron of dizzy moths
did a loop-the-loop
in honour of the PM
and flew straight back in again.

"Hullo"
said a small voice with two bright blue eyes
blinking
at the bottom of the wardrobe.

"Ah. There you are"
said the PM.
"I am the Prime Minister
and very pleased indeed to meet you.

Small Paul emerged
sleepily
to take and shake the PM's outstretched
and down-stretched hand.

"I must have nodded off again.
I am Small Paul
and this
is my bedroom."

"And what a fine bedroom it is!
But do I not detect
the faintest hint
the merest suggestion
the vaguest shadow
of freshly obliterated
footprints
on the walls?"

For his eyesight,
being a self-survived,
seriously suspicious,
near-and-far-sighted
perspicacious politician,
was much better,
much more penetrating
than was Lucybelle's.

"They're my footprints.
I have been practising you see"
confessed Small Paul
embarrassed and
pinkly blushing.

"Curiouser and curiouser"
quoted the Prime Minister.

"Can you keep a secret?"
whispered Small Paul.

"Secrets?
My dear young fellow,
I have filing cabinets
full of secrets."

"Well
my secret is
that
I am a wall walker,"
and he told the tale
of the weeny genie
and the bottle
and the cork
and the spell.

"Here,
I'll show you how it's done,"
and he bent down
to whisper words into
his underpants.

The PM was enthralled
to see Small Paul
tap dancing
on the wall.

"I say
that's frightfully good"
he said.

"My word!
"Perhaps I should take some notes,"
and he hastily scribbled
with a HB pencil
in his Prime Ministerial notebook.

"This could come in handy
one of these fine days."

Then he told Small Paul
about his plan
to do something for the average family.

"What would you suggest?"

"Well, I'm very tired of being stuffed
into this wardrobe,"
sighed Small Paul.
"Perhaps you could do something
about that."

"Mnnn. Let me see"
mused the PM.

"Ah!
At last I have it.
Brilliant!
I shall abolish
wardrobes."

Small Paul clapped with glee.

"And I shall start at once."

And lickety split
quick as two winks
he was out the door
into his limo
and off
in a cloud of bulldust
and sandwich wrappers
while the Smiths,
one man,
one wife,
and
two and a half children,
waved a fond farewell
with fresh tea towels
from their kitchen window.

As the PM
sped through the countryside
he
earnestly
and hastily
scribbled into his notebook
A Bill for the Abolition of Wardrobes
and then he read it
twice.

As soon as he reached
his Lower House
he rang the bells
and announced
to a startled Parliament
the third reading
of
A Bill for the Abolition of Wardrobes.

"Unfair"
screeched the front and back benchers
of the Opposition.
"We haven't read it."

"Well I have,
and I've read it twice,"
said the PM,
and he began to read it again.

"Whereas wardrobes
are a serious health hazard
for very small boys
and provide refuge
for dizzy moths,
this is a Bill
for an Act
to abolish wardrobes throughout the land."

There was immediate uproar
in the House.
Words such as
'nonsense'
'rubbish'
'bizarre'
and
'unfair to moths'
were bandied about
and flew
like a flock in a fluster
this way and that.

"Order. Order.
The House will come to order"
spluttered the Speaker.

"Put him in prison.
Get him a warder"
shouted the Leader of the Opposition.

"Stuff the little microbe
into the wardrobe"
suggested the Shadow Minister for Health and Sterile Dressings.

"Do something.
Do something"
quavered the crotchety Speaker.

And the Prime Minister
ever resourceful in a crisis
decided to demonstrate
his Parliamentary
superiority and
authority.

He bent down
and above the bedlam
of the House
he shouted
into his underpants.

"Jump like a frog
Leap like a flea
Walking on walls
is the thing for me.
Jiggle my jinker
Stifle a stinker
Skiller merinka ree."

He was immediately seen
to leave the despatch box
gently float above the sand glasses
levitate beyond the Speaker's chair
and wave
with his spotted handkerchief
as he passed the public gallery.

"Fraud"
yelled the Shadow Minister for Truth in Sentences.

"Hot air"
yelled the Shadow Minister for Toy Balloons.

And as the Prime Minister
reached the picture rail
above the portrait of the Queen
he began a slow waltz
across the polished paneling
yodeling.

The Shadow Minister for Silly Walks
could think of nothing better
to shout
than
"You're out of time
out of tune
and out of touch."

"Well come up here
and do better"
responded the Prime Minister
thumbing his nose.

This was too much.
This was more than they could bear.
And the Opposition
attacked their tormentors
with rolled-up notice papers
and grubby copies of
Parliamentary Proceedings.

The Sergeant-at-Arms
was so alarmed
he went home to dinner.

"I shall name the members of the Opposition,"
warned the furious Speaker.
And he did,
in alphabetical order what's more,
punctuated by interruptions
from
the Shadow Minister for Interjections.

"I name
Adam, Barnaby, Cuthbert, and Dexter …"

"Shame."

"… Emilio, Felton, Gunther, and Hugh …"

"Shame again."

"… Ivan, Joshua, Kerry, and Luke…"

"Triple shame."

"…Mitchell, Norris, Oliver, and Patterson…"

"Outrageous shame."

"…Quentin, Randy, Sebastian, and Tucker,
Ulverstone, Victor, Warwick, Xavier, Yelverton, and Zachary."

Then
the Leader of the House
moved
that all the Opposition
be suspended
in the air
until they knew
who was boss.

The Leader of the Opposition
was beside himself
with indignation,
his most radical position.
He was red in the face
and frothing at the mouth.
Not a pretty sight.

"That's it.
All my chaps out,"
he shouted.

And like a good Leader
he led them,
his Chief Whip,
all his Shadows
with their shadow cabinet
and the golf trophies,
his private secretaries
and tea ladies,
his hairdresser
and make-up artist,
his driver
and his gym instructor
in his gym shorts,
all in high dudgeon

and low self esteem
down the Parliament steps
across the Prime Minister's pademelon paddock
to a nearby llama farm
where they all …

except for the giggly llamas
and the tickly llama farmer …

where they all
lived
unhappily
ever
after.

Eventually
the Prime Minister
was persuaded to come down
from the picture rail,
and
Lucybelle
sold the wardrobe
for firewood.

The moths
went to live
in a homburg
in a hat box.

And
Small Paul
was appointed
Honorary Minister for Very Small Funny Business
and Changing Light Globes.

And they all lived
ever so happily
ever after.

Paul Drakeford 149 Eglinton Street Kew Victoria Australia
03 9853 1263
belami@netspace.net.au

www.ingramcontent.com/pod-product-compliance
Lightning Source LLC
Chambersburg PA
CBHW061129070526
44584CB00033B/4267